#BEINSPIRED

Dear Omon,

I can truly say that no one
has inspired me the way
you have done (in the last 3-4
years of my life)

I am grateful for you

I am honoured and thankful
for all you've done for me
(by God's grace.)

And I love you,
sister-friend

ADEBOLA ADISA

Adebola Adisa
26022022.
xx

First published in 2022

ISBN 9798771448657

APPRECIATION

I am grateful for social media platforms because they have become forums to connect with my readers.

I thank everyone who has in the past encouraged me to write and all who keep doing so!

I also thank Claire Ogah of Overlaycouture Limited for the cover design.

DEDICATION

I dedicate my third book, #Beinspired, to all

aspiring authors, you too can write!

To all my readers, thank you for believing in me.

To Orinayo and Mo, my forever blessings.

Contents

Foreward

Adebola Adisa is one of the most versatile writers I know. I first met Adebola Adisa in our family physician virtual platform, and we connected because of her personality and character. Adebola is always willing to educate and empower others with knowledge and information, and she has been a major source of inspiration to me and many others.

My first meeting with Adebola Adisa had a significant impact on my life. I remember how thrilled at being in the presence of a woman who had written two books at that time, whilst juggling a busy medical career, motherhood and running a non-profit organisation, amongst many other hats she wears. Suffice it to say that I know Adebola Adisa both personally and professionally. She has authored four more books since then.

Everyone can benefit from reading Adebola Adisa's book #BEINSPIRED. No matter where you are in your life. Whether you need some general guidance, lifestyle advice, or success principles, or you are feeling down, unmotivated, uninspired, or afraid of what the future might hold, Adebola Adisa has a word that would help you #BEINSPIRED.

Not only is Adebola one of the most selfless health advocates and educators I know, but she is also her authentic self and has overcome immense adversities. As you read through Adebola's Adisa's book #BEINSPIRED, there will be things you have heard before, but they have never been presented the way they are in this life-transforming book. This book is less like reading and more like having an experience for your life in different dimensions, including health, lifestyle, inspiration, upliftment, and much more. For me, this book is so inspiring, but at the same time, thought-provoking.

I encourage everyone to read this amazing book and #BEINSPIRED. Adebola's book will be a powerful addition to anyone's library, especially if you are a lover of living holistically. Filling our minds with positive, motivational, inspiring, clear words is an essential part of our journey through life. Adebola Adisa is not only great at helping people tackle their health and mental wellbeing but is also entertaining with this book. Adebola Adisa is not just a writer but also an advocate for holistic living, and she encourages everyone to be their best self – physically and mentally.

    #BEINSPIRED is a fresh, bold attempt at empowering people to live holistically abundant lives unapologetically. #BEINSPIRED reminds us to believe in ourselves, to be health-conscious, adopt the right mindset and live our best lives.

It is with honour that I write this foreword because it is true.

You must #BEINSPIRED!

Dr Omon Imohi

Introduction

#Beinpired is my third book.

Over the past year, I have found myself drawn to write on social media.

I have felt a responsibility to help steer people away from health-related myths and stereotypes that have hitherto been passed down to several generations and to ours.

My passion for writing, and my degree in Medicine, and ongoing experience as a primary care physician

(Family doctor/GP) gives me the appropriate foundation and skills.

I hope that you will also find inspiration from my quotes and poetry.

Do have a great time reading and learning.

But there is a spirit in man: and the inspiration of the Almighty giveth them understanding.

Job 32 : 8 (KJV)

Part 1; Healthy Living

Part one consists of writings about topical issues such as

healthy lifestyle, men's health, breast cancer,

cervical cancer screening and mental health conditions such

as depression and dementia.

#BEINSPIRED

I Can See Clearly Now

I can see clearly now!

I always wanted to wear prescription eyeglasses.

My craving to wear one became even more intense

when my younger brother got his.

I recall how I would tell my dad that I couldn't read

what the teacher wrote on the blackboard at school.

So, we ended up at the Opticians countless times,

but I was always caught out, even when I pretended

that I couldn't read the letters displayed on those

lighted screens.

I am sure that I'm not alone. Who else did this?

Back to the present, I now finally have my wish,

though genuine this time, yet I often don't

remember to put my glasses on. I even tried contact lenses at

some point, and loved them, for a while!

Okay so, when last did you have your eye check.

Did you know that your prescriptions change from time to time if you already wear glasses that is?

The average recommended time to have your eye check is about every two years.

If you are straining to see clearly or your vision is all blurry, I think it's time to visit your Optician, don't just buy glasses from the roadside or a store.

Straining your eyes is one of the common causes of headaches, but there are several other causes of headaches too.

Eye problems are a pointer to different health problems in our body.

If you're experiencing any problems with your eyes, please visit your doctor as soon as possible.

If you already have prescription glasses, don't forget to put them on as recommended, either for reading only or everyday use.

I have found that it makes a lot of difference.

To those who still wish to wear glasses at all costs, don't fret, be patient, as you might get your wish too!

Toothcare

I once cried from pain when I had a toothache.

I actually remember crying!

I was unable to do anything else until I saw the Dentist.

It was a constant throbbing pain.

Nothing seemed to help it get better.

Well, except warm salty water.

Thanks to my Dentist who did his thing.

I was much better in no time.

To avoid ending up like me one day.

You do need to take good care of your teeth.

Here are the dos and don'ts.

• Attend regular appointments with your Dentist.

• Use toothpaste with fluoride content.

• Brush your teeth last thing before bedtime and at least one other time .e.g. before or after breakfast.

• Avoid brushing immediately after eating.

• After brushing, don't rinse your mouth, instead you should spit out the excess toothpaste.

• Floss regularly after meals(I must confess that I struggle with this, but it is essential).

• Stop smoking.

• Cut down on sugary food and drinks.

• Cut down on, or if possible, avoid sweets, chocolates, and their

  likes.

• If eating or drinking anything sugary .e.g. treats, take them during mealtimes.

• Change your toothbrush regularly (at least every 3 to 4 months or when the bristles are no longer upright or appear splayed, whichever occurs earlier).

If you have tooth problems, go, and see your Dentist asap, not your family doctor or GP.

There's a reason these brilliant people spent five, six years or more studying how to help your teeth stay healthy or get better!

Nosebleeds

In most cases, nose bleeds are not a sign of serious illness, and can be managed at home.

Common causes of nosebleeds.

• Picking your nose
• Change in the weather/temperature causing dryness in your nose
• Sneezing hard or blowing your nose hard
• Some medications

Seeing yourself or anyone else bleeding from the nose can no doubt be scary.
However, try not to go into panic mode.

Here's what to do.

- Sit or stand upright
- Lean your head forward
- Do not lie down
- Breath through your mouth
- Try not to swallow the blood as it may cause you to vomit
- Pinch the soft area above your nostrils together for 10 to 15 minutes
- Apply a pack of ice(covered by a towel) over your nose

Check out this link for a video of what to do if you have a nosebleed.

https://youtu.be/PmmhxW0vVXA

Video courtesy of St John's Ambulance.

Attend the Emergency Department if

- You have been bleeding for about 20 minutes
- You had a head injury just before the nosebleed
- You have had heavy nose bleeding or vomited from

swallowing blood

- You feel breathless or are unwell following the nosebleed, or you have been ill before that.
- In any child younger than two years

Go and see your usual doctor if

- You have been getting a lot of nose bleeds(this may be a sign of underlying illness)
- You are on blood-thinning medications
- You have health conditions that affect your body's ability to clot

Key Points

Do not panic

Watch the video on how to stop nose bleeds then you will know how to help yourself and others

Avoid picking your nose

If your nose feels dry, you can use emollients such as Vaseline to moisten it

Vaccines

Vaccines are a necessity!

Flashback to a few weeks ago when my daughter developed a rash which to my trained eyes appeared to be Measles.

However, I questioned the diagnosis because it did not fit.

So, we saw her doctor for a second opinion, and he questioned it even more.

We agreed that it was unlikely to be since she was adequately vaccinated.

Thankfully, soon enough she was better.

Make no mistake, measles can be deadly.

Now, imagine if she was not vaccinated, as the anti-vaxxers would prefer everyone not to be.

Anti-vaxxers, are people who, without evidence, say that vaccines cause medical conditions such as Autism and Infertility.

They hide under the guise of intellect, religion, and the power of social media.

But we know better.

We know that vaccines are gifts.

Legacies bequeathed to us all by science and research.

There is good evidence that vaccines are safe and effective if given appropriately.

In the first five years of life, children are susceptible to many infections and diseases.

Common childhood infections which vaccines protect against include measles, mumps, rubella, tetanus, polio, tuberculosis, hepatitis, whooping cough, meningitis and many more.

Some of these infections though deadly, thankfully are preventable with appropriate vaccination.

Vaccines work by helping the body's defences to develop immunity, thus protecting it if exposed to that specific disease later. This process is called immunisation.

The first group of vaccines are given in the first four to six weeks of life.

This may vary slightly depending on where you live.

In some places, babies are vaccinated with oral polio vaccine and BCG (which protects against tuberculosis).

Vaccines help to protect your child and other children through a process known as 'herd immunity' If your child is not vaccinated, you are not just denying your child that extra protection but could be putting other children at risk too.

The essential vaccines are free of cost to every child so that money would not be an obstacle. Children may experience side effects, but these are usually mild, lasting only a few hours or days.

Your health care provider will advise you about likely side effects and what you need to do.

Remember that your child is counting on you to give them the best chance at living a healthy life.

What can you do?

Find out about the immunisation schedule in your country (check your child's red book if you live in the UK).

Ensure that your child is up to date with their vaccines(check your child's red book for any outstanding vaccines if you live in the UK)

This responsibility is yours as a parent.

Please do not leave that responsibility or expectation to others(including your health professionals).

If you have daughters, find out about the vaccines which protect against cervical cancer.

Remember other vaccines such as the yearly flu vaccine where applicable (this depends on where you live)

Remember that children are the future!

Let us give them the best chance.

Antibiotics Resistance

A few years ago, I volunteered to become an Antibiotic Guardian.

Hopefully, this write-up is part of me fulfilling this role.

Antibiotics are sometimes called antibacterials or antimicrobials.

The first Antibiotic known as Penicillin was discovered by a British scientist, Alexander Fleming in, 1928.

The most recent Antibiotic was discovered in 1987, over 30 years ago.

Antibiotics usually work by killing Bacteria bugs or limiting their spread or multiplication. They are available as liquids, tablets, capsules, creams, ointments, and injections.

An infection is the invasion of our body by disease-causing agents such as Viruses, Bacteria and Fungi.

Let us call these 'Bugs'

When attacked by bugs, our body's army system can defend itself, and within a few days, sometimes lasting several weeks, we get back to normal.

Most of the common cold, cough, ear, eye, and throat symptoms that we develop, are caused by viruses and fall into the category referred to as self-limiting illnesses.

We must avoid taking Antibiotics unless prescribed because they are only effective against bacterial infections and not viruses.

Another reason to avoid taking Antibiotics without prescription is that they can cause harmful side effects. One could also be allergic to specific ones such as Penicillins, which may have fatal consequences.

The greatest concern about the indiscriminate use of Antibiotics is the occurrence of Antibiotic resistance.

Over time, the over-prescription and overuse of Antibiotics have allowed some of the bacteria bugs to become superbugs such that the readily available and cost-effective Antibiotics do not kill them.

Imagine that someone has a chest infection, and no antibiotics can cure them, they will continue to be sick and may die.

So, be your brother's keeper, don't borrow Antibiotics

prescribed to your friend or family member.

Stop buying Antibiotics over the internet, open markets or from unapproved chemists or pharmacies.

Please do not take any Antibiotics when it is not prescribed to you by your doctor.

If your doctor prescribes antibiotics, take them exactly as prescribed and for the total number of days.

Health professionals also need to be careful and must be able to justify Antibiotic prescriptions.

Remember that if we are not careful to use them appropriately, everyone in the world, young and old, may no longer have any effective Antibiotics available when we need them.

Can You Eat Your Cake and Have it?

This morning, I went out for a jog, alone!

I enjoy running outdoors. I do!

But now and then, I still get a couple of obstacles along my path.

They are time(lack of) and boredom(more of impatience)!

None of which are good enough excuses!

To run at least three times a week, I must do a part of it alone, which I don't enjoy doing.

Back then to, this cake-eating business.

5Km, about 30 minutes later, and in fact during my jog, I was able to put together the thoughts for this write-up

Yesterday my sister brought back this massive cake from Cakebox, and I know without a doubt that I'm going for almost half of it.

Hopefully to be devoured over this next week.

I wouldn't call myself a sweet tooth all year round, but mine is what I call a seasonal habit.

Or am I kidding myself!

Anyway, I now need to burn enough calories to fit in all the ones from the cake.

Talk about a motivating factor!

I don't even have the guts to check the total calorie content yet, but I know that I must do so as soon as possible.

Please wish me well!

So back to calorie counting.

For the most part, our weight is the balance of what we eat and drink minus what we burn(through our daily activities and exercises)

If we eat more than we burn, we add on weight.

For me, it's a daily struggle.

I have a digital bathroom scale which I use almost every morning.

Over the last year since I began regular exercises, I've seen how I could gain anything between 0.5 to 2kg, sometimes over 24 hours!

I have found out that I can lose weight if I put my mind to it, but I can also gain it back if I don't eat carefully.

The important thing is to know yourself, know your body, know you, know what works for you!

Try to eat a well-balanced diet with lots of fruits, vegetables, protein and less carbohydrates and starch.

Drink plenty of water.

Don't be an excessive sweet tooth.

Avoid Stress.

Incorporate exercises into your routine; walking, jogging, running, gym, swimming, skipping, it's an endless list.

All in all, do the best thing for you but try and ensure that your choice is to live a healthy lifestyle.

You will thank yourself later.

Stay healthy, friends!

Body Mass Index (BMI)

Many of us struggle with our weight.

BMI is the acronym for Body Mass Index

It translates as; how much weight our height carries.

Imagine constantly carrying a container containing 1 litre of water around in your tummy or on your heart.

Imagine the strain that it will cause to your body.

You calculate BMI by dividing your weight in kilograms by your height in metres squared.

As adults, our height, for the most part, is fixed, but the variable here is our weight.

So, let's do some Arithmetic, enters in BODMAS.

To calculate your BMI, you can use the link below.

https://www.nhs.uk/live-well/healthy-weight/bmi-calculator

Interpret your results as below.

Underweight: less than 18.5

Healthy weight: between 18.5-24.9

Overweight: between 25-29.9

Obese: between 30-39.9

PS: link courtesy of the NHS Website

(Note that some countries use different values)

Obesity puts us at high risk of developing diseases such as Hypertension, Diabetes, Stroke and Heart Attack.

Indeed, there is evidence that weight loss reduces the risk of developing diabetes, especially for those in the high-risk group known as Prediabetes.

Whilst there may be various ways of losing weight and attaining the highly desirable healthy BMI range, the major keys are the two Es.

Eat Healthily

Exercise

What can you do now?

• Calculate your BMI

• Eat healthily

• Exercise regularly

• Speak to your doctor if your BMI is not within the healthy

range.

Stay healthy!

Physical Fitness

Our bodies are designed to move!

Are you familiar with the term 'sedentary lifestyle'?

Are you also familiar with the concept of 10,000 steps a day?

Seems easy to achieve, doesn't it? Well, no, not really!

I found out that the most steps that I can do during a normal workday seeing my patients are just over 4000 steps, even if I go to the waiting room to call them.

A deliberate effort is needed to achieve adequate and regular physical activity!

Physical fitness is a state of health and well-being. It is the ability to actively engage in exercises and day to day physical activities.

To maintain good health, two types of physical activities are important

1. Aerobic exercises

2. Muscle-strengthening exercises

The WHO recommends that all adults between 18 to 64 years should participate in at least 150 minutes a week of moderate-intensity, or 75 minutes a week of vigorous-intensity aerobic physical activity, or a combination of moderate-intensity and vigorous-intensity aerobic activity in equivalent amounts.

The level of intensity is important and must increase the heartbeat and make you sweat.

In addition to this, an adult should do exercises that work all the major muscles, on 2 or more days a week.

And what's not to like, seeing that there are so many benefits!

Types of Exercises

Walking

Jogging

Running

Swimming

Cycling

Martial Arts

Dancing

Other sports include tennis, badminton, football, volleyball etc.

How to Exercise

• Choose an activity such as running/jogging/walking or any sport.

• Decide to start.

• If the notion of running scares you, you could start with walking.

• Be determined to do it.

• Decide on your start date.

• Plan your routes.

• Be flexible.

• Find a group near you and if you cannot find one, start one!

• Get comfortable gear (vest, bottoms, sports bra where applicable, socks, shoes, water bottle). A fitness watch or similar device won't hurt, and these do not have to be expensive.

• On D Day, be ready on time and start.

• Start slowly.

- Do gentle warm-ups before and cool down after each session.
- To begin, do not set any time pressure or targets. It could come later.
- Stop if you feel breathless or feel too tired to continue.
- Aim for two or three sessions a week and gradually build this up.
- Always have your water handy and stay well hydrated.
- To avoid getting bored, you could change your routes regularly.
- Gradually increase your pace and distance. For instance, you could brisk-walk.
- The key is consistency, and soon you will find out how easy it is.
- It may help to find a way to include it in your routine. e.g. during school runs or lunch break.
- Stay safe and well protected from the weather/ elements!
- There are several free apps and exercise plans available

online. Why not check them out to see what best suits you?

The Health-Conscious Man

There are many reasons why men may delay visits to their doctor, even when they are aware that something isn't quite right.

1. They may be busy being busy

A man may be doing all he can to cater for his family and trying to give them the best of everything. As a result, he may not find the time to take care of his health.

2. Fear of the unknown

A man may be having health issues but may be too scared of the possible diagnosis and prefers to ignore his symptoms, hoping that they never become worse or that the problem would disappear.

3. Macho attitude/ Mr Hulk Hogan.

A man may trivialize his symptoms or have a higher pain threshold and may cope better with his symptoms.

4. The protective Man

A man may not want to bother his loved ones and may keep his health issues a secret to protect loved ones or because he doesn't want them to be worried.

These are all genuine reasons!

However, there are more important reasons why men should not ignore their health issues.

If you are gone, your loved ones who you have been protecting may never be able to get over your loss, and you may end up leaving them vulnerable.

You may have a treatable health condition such as Hypertension and Diabetes, which you may not be aware of, but these may put you at risk of developing conditions such as heart attack or Stroke.

If you take good care of your health, you have a better chance of being a better and present son, husband, dad, brother, uncle, friend, and colleague!

If you are aged 40 and over, it is time to get your regular health check with your doctor.

Remember that a health-conscious man is a responsible man!

Still on Men's Health

It is common knowledge that men often delay visits to their doctor, even when they know that something is not quite right.

Health problems affecting men include Depression, High blood pressure, Diabetes, Stroke, Heart attack, erectile dysfunction and urinary tract and prostate problems.

Let us look at these key numbers.

- 37; a waist size of 37 inches or above puts you at higher risk of heart disease, stroke, diabetes, and cancer.
- 150; aim for 150 minutes of physical activity a week.
- 5; aim to eat 5 portions of fruit and vegetables every day.
- 14; do not take any more than 14 units of alcohol a week and avoid more than 6 units per day(binge drinking)
- 10; cigarette smokers die 10 years younger than non-smokers.
- 120/80 mmHg and below is the ideal blood pressure.

Ensure that you get your blood pressure checked because hypertension often gives no signs.

• 75% of suicides are by men.

Well-man clinics for men aged 40 and over

These are clinics where men can get something akin to an MOT.

Note that this may not be free.

Your doctor can do the following.

• Discuss your lifestyle, including diet, exercise, alcohol, and smoking.

• Check your weight and height to calculate your BMI.

• Check your blood pressure.

• Routine blood tests including cholesterol, thyroid, blood sugar.

• Do a urine test to check for urine infections or kidney problems.

• Do an electrocardiogram (ECG) to check for heart problems

- Do a chest X-ray if you are a heavy smoker.
- Advise on cancers that can affect men, testicular and prostate cancer.

What can you do?

- Find out if your doctor can arrange a well-man check for you.
- See your doctor immediately you feel unwell, leaving it till later may be too late.
- Eat healthily.
- Exercise regularly.
- Stop smoking.
- Cut down on alcohol.
- Get adequate sleep.
- Drink enough water.
- Ensure that you take your prescribed medications as advised.

Be a healthy man!

Cervical Screening

Growing up, like most children, I was curious and remember rummaging through my mum's makeup, clothes, books, and other stuff and finding her Pap smear result.
I am not even sure why this memory has stuck with me!
The cervical screening test checks the health of the lining of the neck of the womb, the cervix.
The cervix is the area which when fully dilated to 10cm, allows a baby to pass through during the process of labour and delivery.
Smears are offered to women between the ages of 20 and 65(this differs from place to place).

Facts

• Cervical cancer though not a sexually transmitted disease, occurs in sexually active women.
  It occurs because of the spread of certain viruses through sex.

- Cervical cancer is mostly preventable if pre-cancerous cells are detected early and removed.
- Cervical screening is not 100% accurate and does not prevent all cases of cervical cancer, but when done, it significantly reduces the incidences of cervical cancer.
- They are not one-off tests and must be done at regular intervals.

At the appointment

- You may wish to take along a friend or relative and, you do not need to be scared.
- The whole procedure usually takes about 5 to 10 minutes. It is easier and quicker when you are relaxed
- Your health professional will discuss what the test is. Remember to ask any questions that you have. Try not to be embarrassed because your health professional is a professional and has done this countless times. Ask for a woman if you prefer.
- Some people experience some discomfort or light bleeding after, but only for a few days. Please see your health professional if you are concerned.

Test Results

- Results are usually ready in 2 weeks
- Most results return as normal.
  Always check when your next smear test is due(please attend this)
- Some results show abnormal changes which may require further tests or treatment, and your doctor should refer you to specialists.
- Some smear tests need to be redone(usually if the sample is inadequate)

Booking your appointment

- Try to book an appointment for when you are not on your period (usually about fourteen days from the start of your last period)
- No earlier than three months after you had your last baby
- At least 24 hours after using a spermicide, barrier method of contraception, or lubricant jelly.

Are you up to date with your cervical smear?

Find out if your mum, sister, BFF, and colleagues are up to date with theirs?

If not, do encourage them to be!

Don't leave it until it is too late.

Find out where your nearest testing centre is or see your GP or family doctor to book your smear test today.

Know Yourself,
Breast Examination

I have always believed that it's almost impossible for anyone else to know you more than you know yourself.

Let's talk about breast examination.

Self-breast examination aka SBE.

It is important to check your breasts and armpits.

The usual advice is to do this at least once a month.

When you make this a routine, it's more likely that you will notice any changes early.

There are different types of changes in the breast, and these may include a lump in the breast or armpit, a dimple in the skin of the breast or nipple discharge.

But there may be other changes that I have not listed.

Changes in the breast may be signs of breast cancer, but they may not be.

If you notice any change in your breast or are concerned about their appearance, it is best to see your doctor immediately.

It is normal to be scared at this time, but whatever you do, please do not keep it to yourself!
Ignoring it won't make it go away.

Please don't resort to taking herbs or concoction.

Please don't allow a traditional doctor to make cuts or incisions on it.

Please don't just stay at home or in a religious house only praying about it.

God has equipped health professionals to help you get better.

If you are someone who prays, then in addition to seeing your doctor, you could also then pray that God will grant your doctors all the wisdom and skills to get you better.

Pray also that science will find a cure to all forms of cancer soon.

Breast Cancer is real, and early detection is very crucial because it gives one a better chance of being a survivor because it's easier to treat then.

What can you do?

1. DO regular Self-breast examination.

   Here is the link on how to do this.

   https://www.breastcancer.org/pictures/self_exam

2. DO NOT ignore the changes.

3. If you notice any changes, DO see your doctor IMMEDIATELY.

4. DO offer support to anyone you know who has breast cancer, it is a tough journey.

5. DO support causes and charities that are trying to find a cure.

   Do not forget that men can have breast cancer too!

   Check those breasts, act today, act now!

Mammograms;
Breast Cancer Screening

Mammograms are X-ray tests that help detect breast cancer.

In England, it is offered to every woman between ages 50 and 71 and usually done every three years. It may be commenced earlier, later, or more regularly depending on the individual risk of developing breast cancer.

In some other places, you may have to pay for it.

Pros

Mammograms may detect breast cancers before a lump is felt in the breast.

It is more likely to detect breast cancer if it is already present.

It is often a quick and simple test to have done.

Cons

It may be less effective if you have breast implants and in younger women, as they have denser breast tissue.

It may not detect all breast cancers even if they were already present.

It may also put one at risk of radiation (albeit low at each visit) as well as having invasive tests and treatment where the condition detected may not have caused any problem or threatened life (had it not been detected)

What happens when you attend a Mammogram appointment?

Once all your details are checked, the mammographer (the specialist who takes the Xray's) may ask a few questions.

Ensure that your mammographer is aware if you are pregnant or breastfeeding.

The Mammogram may need to be postponed as X-rays may be harmful to your baby.

Then, you will need to undress from waist up (including removing your bra)

It may be helpful if you could wear a top and bottom, instead of a dress.

This is only for your convenience.

Then the Mammographer will place your breasts on the X-ray machine and lower a clear plastic plate unto it to flatten your breast. When this is done, you may feel a squeeze and some discomfort in your breast, but this should be short-lived.

At that stage, you will need to stay still and hold your breath very briefly whilst the pictures are taken, one breast at a time.

Everything is likely to be completed within 30 minutes.

You may wish to take a friend along, but they would not be able to stay in the same room with you when the X-ray is being done.

Results

You will usually get your results within two weeks, and in some cases much earlier.

Possible results (England).

Normal in most instances; so, you go back to the three-yearly recall.

Unclear results: you may need to repeat the mammogram. About 1 in 25 women may be asked to come for further tests. This does not always imply that you have breast cancer.

About 1 in 100 women will be diagnosed with breast cancer after more detailed assessments and tests.

Other key facts

Mammograms are screening tests and therefore having it done does not imply that one will not develop breast cancer.

So, if you already have abnormal lumps or noticed any abnormalities in your breasts, it is important to see your GP immediately(even if you have had a mammogram recently)

Regular(at least monthly) self-breast examinations are important.

Remember that early detection of breast cancer offers a better chance for prompt treatment and a better chance of survival.

PS

If you need to arrange your Mammogram privately, ensure that you attend a reputable and certified provider.

Infertility;
Speaking from Experience

My husband and I waited for seven years before we had our first child.

Infertility is when couples are not able to achieve pregnancy despite regular unprotected sex for at least a year.

Let us break it down a bit.

Regular unprotected sex here refers to having sex without protection(condoms, femidoms, contraceptive caps etc.)

It must occur about thrice a week(at least 2 or 3 days apart)

Almost like the law of diminishing returns, the more you try, the harder it seems.

In addition to this, the longer the wait to become pregnant, the harder and more disinterested one may become at having sex.

It is ironic, for without sex, there would not be any pregnancy at all!!!

Speaking from personal experience, it is tough waiting and hoping to become pregnant.

Even though medically speaking, one must have waited up to a year before being termed infertility, the reality of waiting for even a few months can be stressful.

Waiting one day more than one desires to have a child can be devastating.

It can also make one feel very anxious and depressed.

One can devote everything, time, money etc., in search of an answer and completely ignore every other area of life, yet it may never happen.

You are likely to become vulnerable and gullible.

It happened to me!

I lost time and sacrificed a lot, my confidence, peace, focus, dreams, friendships and so on, on the altar of infertility.

My life PAUSED!

It was a low point in my life.

There is the added pressure and the assumption that the blame must solely lie with the woman.

This is a sign of ignorance and demonstrates the lack of public awareness about the causes of infertility.

Can I quickly point out to couples, their family, and friends, that it is pointless to blame anyone because it will not make things better.

It is also cruel to do so.

I wanted what I wanted so much, and no one could make it happen.

You see, the search for having children is one aspect of life that may defy logic, time, money, faith, and everything else.

Somehow, I survived!

How did I survive?

My understanding husband.

Supportive parents, siblings, and in-laws(especially my mother-in-law)

Relocation away, from where the pressure was likely to come.

Seeking answers early, through medicine.

Seeking answers through my faith.

Reading and watching other people's stories.

Preparing for the worst outcome of having no biological children.

I considered the option of adoption.

The singular most important decision(I think) that I made was to **FOCUS ON GETTING ON WITH MY LIFE!!!**

It took so long and, I only managed to reach this step about five years later.

PS

Can I quickly say that there is no one size fits all.
Do what you must do(legally and within reason) to survive?

Vaginal Douching

I am clean!

Douching is the process of washing, soaking, or cleaning the vaginal area by squirting plain water or water mixed with homemade remedies or over the counter (OTC) preparations.

These preparations are varied and may include lemon, vinegar, and baking soda.

The aim is to clean out perceived dirt from the vaginal area.

Some people use special bottles or syringes to douch.

Now, douching is different from simple washing or rinsing the vagina with clean water(only) during a bath or shower.

Simple cleaning is good as our vagina protects itself and does not require you to clean it overzealously.

Isn't that just fantastic!

Some women douch because they think they are unclean.

They douch after sex because they feel dirty after.

Dear woman, you are clean!

Repeat after me, I am clean!

Our vagina contains good bacteria called lactobacilli.

The loss of these lactobacilli, .e.g., through douching, allows the overgrowth of non-beneficial bacteria, and this allows the vagina skin to become less acidic and reduces its ability to defend itself against infections.

There's evidence that douching is quite harmful.

• It increases the risk of developing vaginal thrush.

• It increases the risk of developing bacterial vaginosis (BV)

• There is evidence that it allows the infection to travel up the female organs faster, thereby increasing the risk of pelvic infections.

• This may then increase the risk of infertility or ectopic pregnancies.

Do Not Douch

• Before, during or after sex.

• Douching won't cure or prevent vaginal infections but will increase the risk of developing abnormal vaginal discharge.

• Douching will not prevent unwanted pregnancies.

• Douching will not permanently cure any bad vaginal odour.

- Douching will not prevent sexually transmitted infections(STIs) such as HIV infections.
  Current evidence is that women should not douch.
  See your doctor if you have any abnormal vaginal discharge.

Do Not Douch!
Do Not Douch!!
Do Not Douch!!!

Menopause

It's easy to think that Menopause is a misnomer!

Menopause is when a woman's period stops.

This takes place over a few or several years, and usually between ages 45 to 50 years, average 51 years, but could be earlier or later.

A girl child is born with all the eggs that she would need during her lifetime; talk about putting all one's eggs in a basket.

These eggs are released one after the other until the last one, enters MenoStop.

Certain symptoms then occur because of changes in the level of the female hormone called Oestrogen.

These symptoms include

Erratic periods until they finally stop

Hot flushes

Night sweats

Poor sleep

Mood changes

Loss of interest in sex

Discomfort during sex due to vaginal dryness

The severity may vary but may be so severe as to result in a relationship or marital breakdown and believe me this is no joke!

If you're experiencing any of these symptoms, you don't have to suffer in silence, do go and see your family doctor or GP.

They will help make the diagnosis.

Ask them about HRT and non-Hormonal Medications.

Several myths surround the use of HRT, but most of them are neither evidence-based nor true.

HRT means Hormone Replacement Therapy; they are medications that can help settle most of the above symptoms

They come in different forms such as gel, creams, patches, tablets etc.

They can be so effective that women who take them do not want to stop. However, it is best to stop taking them when your doctor advises you to.

Also, be aware that it may not be safe for everyone to be on them.

You also need regular reviews when taking HRT, usually yearly, but check with your doctor to be sure.

There are a few non-hormonal medications, that may also be effective against menopausal symptoms. Ask your local Pharmacist about these.

Maybe your wife, sister, daughter, grandma, friend or colleague or anyone you know is experiencing menopausal symptoms, then it's time to encourage them to see their doctor and support them through this.

Remember that your life does not need to stop because of Menopause.

MenoGo it!

Seizures,

Fits and Convulsions

As a child, I can still recall the chaotic and frightening sight; everyone running up and down, someone pouring cold water and another person trying to force medications or glucose or their fingers in between the gritting teeth of someone having a seizure.

Some of you have witnessed this too!

Seizures are sudden abnormal discharge of electrical activity in the brain that causes the body to respond in that way.

There are various causes.

Apart from Epilepsy, one of the major causes of fits in children is 'febrile convulsion,' that is also known as febrile seizures. It may occur in some children(usually age six months to three years) when they have a fever due to an infection, but in some cases, the cause is not known.

Febrile convulsions are often one-offs, and most children recover without complications.

Epilepsy is a brain condition that leads to frequent seizures/ convulsions/fits.

It is not often curable but, in most cases, can be well managed with medications.

In most cases, the causes are unknown.

However, Epilepsy is **NOT CONTAGIOUS.**

Symptoms

These are involuntary.

Aura: some people sense or have symptoms that make them aware that they will have a seizure just before it happens.

Usually lasts less than five minutes.

Stiffness, twitching or jerking hands and legs

Tongue biting, eye-rolling, foaming in the mouth

Unconsciousness, then they may recover slowly(but may feel drowsy for a while)

They may wet themselves with urine or soil themselves with faeces.

Some people experience seizures that appear different, such as the following.

Loss of awareness about the surroundings and staring blankly into space as if in a trance.

Strange sensations such as a funny sensation in the tummy. Unusual smell or taste or a tingling sensation, in the arms or legs.

Repetitive movements like lip-smacking.

It is important to identify when anyone is having these types of seizures so that you can get help.

Do Not

Do not put anything inside their mouth(water, food, medications, spoons, fingers etc.).

Do not stigmatize them(IT IS NOT contagious).

Do not pour water on them.

Do not abandon or run away from them.

What can you do?

Check that the surroundings are safe and remove any hazards safely(live wire, sharp objects, open fire etc) if you can.

You also need to be safe otherwise, you may be unable to help them.

Put them in the recovery position if you are trained to.

Get them to the doctor immediately.

You need to ring an ambulance(where available) or get them to the hospital immediately if the following happens.

Seizures lasting more than 5 minutes

Head injury

Non-stop bleeding from anywhere

Struggling to breathe.

Diagnosis

An eyewitness account is important(ideally the eyewitness should accompany them to the doctor's appointment, making a note of what happened and how long for)

The doctor will ask questions and examine them as appropriate.

In most cases, no further test is needed to make the diagnosis of a simple febrile convulsion, and there may be no need for medications.

However, if your doctor suspects that it may be Epilepsy, he will arrange further tests and a referral to specialists.

Tests usually include blood and urine tests, brain scans and EEG(electroencephalogram), which shows a tracing of electrical activities in the brain.

Your doctor will refer you to specialists known as Neurologists, and in some cases, you may need to be seen by Neurosurgeons.

Treatment

Medications are the mainstay of treatment for most people and are often lifelong unless otherwise advised by your doctor.

It may take a while for your doctors to get your doses just right, but do not despair.

Some people are managed with surgery and dietary adjustments.

Day to Day Living

Most people can live normal lives if their seizures are well controlled and can be seizure-free for a long time.

What else can you do?

Live a healthy lifestyle.

Be aware of any seizure triggers that you may have, stress, poor sleep, flashing lights, illnesses, excess alcohol, drugs, and medications. Avoid or manage these quickly,

Be aware of safety precautions at home, cooking, bathing, ensure smoke detectors to reduce fire hazards.

Be aware of safety precautions and adjustments at work, especially if operating heavy machinery.

Be aware of safety precautions with sports such as contact sports and swimming.

Be aware of your local driving laws.

Speak to your doctor about contraception if you're in a sexual relationship.

Plan pregnancies carefully and ensure that you engage with appropriate antenatal and postnatal care.

Find out what support you may be entitled to, such as benefits, free prescriptions etc.

Find your local support groups as these are good sources of information.

PS

COMPLIANCE with medications is important.

Remember that **CONVULSIONS** are **NOT CONTAGIOUS**, so you would not have convulsions by helping someone who has Epilepsy.

Let us Stop the Epilepsy/ Convulsion Stigma!

Dementia

Dementia is an ongoing deterioration in brain function, such that it begins to affect a person's day to day life. It is often irreversible.

Advancing age is not the cause of Dementia, though it is more commonly diagnosed in older people(usually over 65) and is also a risk factor.

Other risk factors include

More common in women.

Excess alcohol consumption

Smoking

Hypertension

High cholesterol

History of Stroke.

Parkinson's disease.

Down's syndrome.

Genetic causes.

Types of Dementia

Alzheimer's

Vascular

Mixed Dementia

Dementia with Lewy Bodies

Frontotemporal.

Some symptoms are specific to certain types of Dementia

In general, the early symptoms of Dementia include.

Loss of memory especially new information.

Difficulty concentrating.

Getting confused about doing usual familiar activities,

cooking, handling finances, taking medications etc.

Finding it difficult to follow conversations

Poor judgement.

Being unable to find the appropriate words.

Asking questions repeatedly.

Being confused about time, places, and events.

It is easy to assume that they are deliberately ignoring

important things, or they may appear to be lying.

Mood changes.

The above symptoms may gradually become worse, but some people may deteriorate more quickly.

Symptoms of advanced Dementia

Difficulty in recognising family, friends, and places.

They may wander around and struggle to find their way home.

Difficulty with speech or complete loss of the ability to speak.

Difficulty with or complete loss of the ability to walk.

They may be prone to repeated falls.

Loss of appetite.

Difficulty with or complete loss of the ability to feed or drink safely due to swallowing problems and increased risk of choking.

Weight loss

They may have problems with swallowing medications too.

Disturbed or poor sleep and or nightmares

Mood disorders; Depression, and Anxiety.

They may become more aggressive or experience hallucinations(seeing or hearing things or voices that are not real)

Accidentally wetting themselves with urine and or soiling themselves with faeces.

People with these symptoms may not be aware, but friends and family members are likely to be.

If you are experiencing these symptoms, go and see your doctor.

If you recognise these symptoms in anyone close to you, encourage them to see their doctor.

Encourage them to take someone they trust along as they may forget what they discussed with their doctor.

Diagnosis

Having a formal diagnosis is important. Often the confirmation of the diagnosis encourages acceptance. It also helps in future planning, health care, care plans, health worker interventions, legal matters, wills and decision making.

Initial consultation with your GP or family doctor

It may help to take along a trusted friend or family member. The consultation may involve your doctor asking questions, physical examination, and the completion of a simple questionnaire.

They may have blood and or urine tests.

This initial stage is important because some medical conditions such as Delirium(sudden confusion), Anxiety and Depression may present like Dementia.

If your doctor thinks that you may have Dementia, they will refer you to see specialists, known as Psychiatrists or Geriatricians(Elderly Care Physicians) or a Neurologist(Brain and nerve specialist)

Specialist Consultation involves more specific questions and more detailed questionnaires.

You may also have a brain scan known as an MRI or CT scan.

It may help to write down all your questions and concerns and ask your specialist.

Ask them to explain more about the diagnosis and anything else that is unclear to you. They may also arrange more specialist assessments or follow up clinics.

The specialist will confirm what type of Dementia you have and if it is at the early or late stage.

It is quite important as it helps determine if you are likely to benefit from medications.

Day to Day Care

- Enjoy being you and stay positive.
- Try to maintain an active social life.
- Try to maintain a routine.
- Use alarms, diaries, notes, and reminders.
- Keep lists of helpful telephone numbers, contacts, addresses and emergency contact details.
- Surround yourself with things or activities that you are familiar with, music, memoirs, and photos of loved ones.
- Share your experience with trusted friends and family or others if you feel comfortable doing so.
- Maintain a healthy lifestyle.
- Dosette boxes(medicine organisers) can be helpful as reminders for your regular medications and may help

avoid an overdose.

• Sleep well.

• Depression is common, so ask your doctor for help if you feel low all the time.

• See your doctor promptly if you feel unwell as infections may make your Dementia symptoms worse.

• Ask for help and support from friends, family, health care professionals and support groups.

• Initially, you may be able to continue to live on your own, with support. However, as Dementia progresses, this may become unsafe.

For instance, you may be prone to more falls, fire safety concerns while cooking, getting missing when you leave the house or forgetting to eat and drink.

• You may be able to live with family members but if not you may need to move into a care or nursing home for better care.

In the UK, the social services can arrange a needs assessment which will help identify what your needs are.

Mental Fitness

Many of us live busy lives and have demanding jobs. Burnout, stress, and exhaustion are all terms that we are familiar with and that we might have experienced. Depression and anxiety have no face, regardless of who one is, and are very common.

In a bid to do our best for our loved ones, family members, dependents, friends and at our jobs, it is easy to ignore our own physical and mental health needs. These all seem like recipes for disaster.

We must remember that there is no shortcut to protecting ourselves, and we must find ways to manage our mental wellbeing.

How to maintain your mental wellbeing

· Be registered with a GP/family doctor and attend regular health checks.
· Manage any long-term health conditions, such as

Hypertension and Diabetes by taking your medications regularly and living a healthy lifestyle.

· Know yourself, your limits, and boundaries. Do not take on too much.

· Take regular breaks during each workday, and do not miss lunch.

· Avoid taking work home. Be away from work, in spirit, soul, and body!

· Have a social life or many social lives!

· Have a work mentor.

· Take regular holidays and do not spend your leave doing more work or catching up on any outstanding work. Spend them as a holiday!

· Be versatile because your life is not only about work or earning money through paid employment. Have you thought about maybe owning your own business?

· Be resilient.

· Be prepared to enjoy life without feeling guilty.

· Be financially protected; life insurance, income protection insurance, critical illness insurance, sickness benefits etc.

· Be aware of support networks; family, friends, faith, and mentors and rely on them. Accept their help with day to day needs and depend on them as people you can speak to, who you trust to keep your secret and who can give good advice.

· Recognise when you have had enough, either by your inner voice or the nudge from others, then act on this by pausing or stopping if need be.

· Be proactive in recognising when you are not coping or need help and try to reach out on time. Often, we cannot wish things away, and not acting on time may make things worse.

· Identify your support networks, where and how to reach out to them and do reach out to them.

What is Depression?

So, I have joined the bandwagon of those speaking about depression on social media.

And rightly so because this diagnosis needs to be discussed in a bid to 'demystify' and to 'dejinx' it.

As a family doctor, I see and manage many people with symptoms of depression.

Depression is a state of low mood with symptoms such as feeling sad or hopeless, poor appetite, poor sleep, loss of interest or loss of energy to do things that you would usually love to do, such as work and play.

People who are depressed may cry all the time or are always anxious and afraid and may also have suicidal thoughts and plans.

Other people sleep or eat excessively or are tired all the time.

However, there are other symptoms of depression.

Feeling low about a life change or a life event such as a new sickness diagnosis, loss of a job or loved one may not imply that we are depressed.

People have this reaction to sad events in their lives.

However, if this grief reaction persists beyond a few weeks and is affecting the person adversely, it may mean that they are depressed.

If you feel that you might be going through some or all the above symptoms, or you know someone who is, the best thing to do is to go and see your doctor as soon as possible.

Depression is real!

You don't get it because you are not religious enough or because you are a bad person.

More so, it is unlikely to go away without treatment.

Whereas you can become completely better especially if you start treatment early.

Your treatment may depend on how depressed you are and can be in the form of talking therapies(counselling) and or medications.

People who are depressed need a strong support network of people they trust and love and, this often prevents them from acting on their suicidal thoughts.

Please don't keep it hush-hush!!!

It is not contagious, neither is it a thing of shame or a sin to be depressed.

Seek help now.

Suicide Prevention

In the 120 seconds, it will take to read and digest this write up, 3 people would have died from suicide.

Suicide is when people take their own lives.

Suicide is preventable!

Risk factors

• Mental health conditions like depression and bipolar disorder.

• Excess alcohol and drug misuse.

• Adverse and stressful life changes and loss such as divorce, financial and legal problems, loss of loved ones.

• Military service/ PTSD (Post-traumatic Stress Disorder)

• Family history of suicide.

• Previous suicide attempts.

• Men are more likely to complete suicidal attempts as they often use more lethal means.

• Access to lethal means, Military personnel, Doctors (Anaesthetists)

• Longstanding pain, sickness, and terminal illnesses such

as cancer and history of sexual abuse.

- In children and young people; social media and peer pressure, bullying, and sexual identity problems.

Symptoms

- Always expressing a wish to die or kill yourself.
- Planning how to kill yourself.
- Accessing means to commit suicide, searching online, stockpiling on medications, buying the tools, guns, nooses.
- Isolating yourself.
- Excess alcohol and drugs.
- Putting your affairs in order, saying goodbye to loved ones, giving away belongings, writing suicide notes.
- Hopelessness and preoccupation with dying.

What can you do?

If you think that you may attempt suicide, get help immediately.

- See your doctor or mental health provider.
- Call the CRISIS, Suicide hotlines and your local emergency numbers.

• Speak to family and friends.

• Speak to a mentor, spiritual leader, or trusted others.

How can everyone help?

Increase public awareness about suicide.

Stop the suicide stigma.

Signpost people to their doctor and mental health providers.

Let people know that there is hope and that you care.

PS

Remember that every 40 seconds, someone dies by suicide.

The time to reach out is now!

Ask someone how they are, then ask again to be sure.

#BEINSPIRED

Part 2; Inspirational Titles

In part two, I have written about inspiring and motivational topics such as being confident, not giving up and the benefit of time.

#BEINSPIRED

Become a Confident You

Do you sometimes look at certain people and aspire to have their confidence?

I daresay that some people are born with confidence.

And I am not even joking; it feels like my daughters were born that way. Even at their very young ages, they demonstrate specific confidence in certain areas.

Therefore, parents, guardians, teachers, mentors, and society need to be careful.

Children and younger people can easily have their confidence eroded and may grow up feeling inadequate.

We must be careful to help develop their confidence.

We must help protect and nurture it.

Money, fame, beauty, family connection, profession, intelligence, societal status can certainly bestow confidence on people.

Anything which adds value to us as humans can give us confidence too.

We can develop our confidence.

How can you build self-confidence?

• Believe that you can be a confident you!

• Add to and acquire more value to yourself, for instance, read more, study more, learn new things and experiences, get a new degree or do a new course etc.

  Knowledge is power!

• Look good and dress nice.

  You are addressed the way you dress!

  Remember that you can do this without breaking the bank.

• Surround yourselves with people who encourage you!

• Be friends with people who add more value to you!

• Constantly practise being confident.

• Do not be let down by your past or present failures.

• Be positive and remain so!

• Smile more because it makes you appear like you know what you are doing.

  It sells you!

This is not an exhaustive list.

Maintaining confidence is important too.

Like most things in life, practice makes perfect.

The more we speak, dress, behave and act confident or form confidence, the more people see us as confident.

After a while, we start believing it too, and eventually develop our inner confidence.

There, I encourage you to find your confidence!

Multitasking

Women are awesome at multitasking, we are!

This write up is not about bias.

To the MEN reading, please do not take offence, but I am a woman, and all I know about is women, and we excel at doing several things at the same time.

So, a few weeks back, the scales fell off my eyes. Before then, I always thought that being a Jack of all trades demonstrated a lack of tenacity or determination or even laziness!

Now I know that it isn't, I know better.

I have not come across any woman who cannot multitask and, I think we were born that way.

It is in the DNA!

Women can make dinner, attend to a crying baby, help complete their children's school assignments, be on the telephone encouraging a dear friend, reply to emails, clean up, wash up, load up dirty clothes in the washing machine, fold the clean ones up, bring out the next day's outfit and shoes, whilst still successfully catching up on the evening news, Instagram, and Facebook updates.

If we could do this, then why would it seem strange to have the ability to handle several ideas, concepts, and businesses at the same time.

It is indeed possible to be an excellent full-time housewife with a small business by the side or a big-time CEO who is still present and functional in her kids' life.

Whatever you decide to do, go for it, be it, value it, keep at it, and be excellent in it.

Be you!

So yes, kudos to you, yes you and you and you, dear woman!

A word of advice, do not forget to ask for help, get help, and if you can afford to, pay for it. Do not overburden yourself unnecessarily, you are not a superhero, well not yet, but even if you are one, superheroes need help too!

Facing Rejection

We are all familiar with the Abraham Lincoln story.

Let us bring it closer to home.

Ask Tiger Woods.

This year alone, I have already faced rejection thrice(

probably more times)

In this write-up, I will use rejection loosely to mean failure.

Rejection can be such a sinking feeling!

What can you do?

It is normal to wish to curl up in a little corner, enter the
ground and fade out of existence.

It is okay to do just that; I mean, curl up, but do not
disappear, instead have a good cry.

Accept that it has happened, but more importantly, that it is
a part of life and that it does not signify the end of you, nor
does it dictate your future.

Speak about it and allow your friends and family to
encourage you. Ignore the naysayers. Speak to others who

have similar experiences. Speak to people who buy into your dream.

Learn from it. There is a reason why it happened, and that rejection is unique to you, so own it. Do not ignore it. You conquer by learning from it.

You may learn how not to do what led to the rejection in the first instance.

You may learn how to face rejection, and if it ever happened again, it feels less of a blow.

I passed my UK Driving test on my third attempt. The first time even I knew that I had to fail. At the roundabout in the UK, you give way to traffic on the right. I was not even looking, so the examiner had to break, taking over the driving.

The second time what I did not know was that I had already failed within the first two minutes, because I pointed to the left, but turned right probably out of fear.

I am so grateful that the examiner allowed me to complete the test.

By the third time, I was more confident, more attentive, and more focused under pressure (all of which are skills needed to drive in real life)

Decide if this is a goal that is worth pursuing or just something you happened to have done for the sake of doing it. Like a sudden splash of cold water on the face, the rejection should make you wake up to reality and double-check if this is something you want to do or not.

It may be something you must achieve before you reach the next level, a promotion examination or interview.

It may be something you do not need to or want to do.

It may be something you do not have to do now. Maybe later.

Acquire more tools, experience, education, advice, and skills to be better prepared for the next time. Use time and everything you can harness to garner more ability and power to do it again.

It reminds me of when the plane is going along the runway when it is about to take off, suddenly it **STOPS**, garners more power before **STARTING** again at the top speed that allows it to take off.

Go back and do it again! Yes, do it again!!

It does not mean that you will not face rejection again, and if you do, see it as a cycle that brings you closer to your destination each time.

You become a master haven done it many times already.

The one thing that is common to people who succeed, is that they do not give up.

When you eventually succeed, and you will, if you do not give up, encourage others not to give up too. You can encourage others to face and conquer rejection too.

In this way, you would come full circle and truly face and conquer rejection.

Where Are You Originally From?

One of the questions that Black and minority people often get asked in the Diaspora is this.

'Where are you originally from?'

Notice the emphasis on originally!

Other questions include.

How long have you been here?

Or you get a statement like you speak good English!

On the other hand, how this question is perceived may vary depending on the person asking, the circumstances, who is being asked and the context in which it is being asked.

At times you get the feeling that it is a rhetoric question, a matter-of-fact statement that immediately puts you in your 'place' and lets you know that you are not one of 'them'.

At other times you feel that it is a question born out of genuine curiosity.

Yet at other times you know that the person asking feels a connection to you; may have been to your land of birth, or have friends from there, and may even be married to someone or have other family members and in-laws from there.

At times it is just an ice breaker because the person asking does not know how else to begin a conversation with you. This last reason is the one I suggest that people replace with another question like ' isn't the weather lovely today or something.

In the United Kingdom, talking about the weather is a good ice breaker, certainly better than asking someone where they are from.

Moreover, it is not a fair question.

As you often do not feel that you can ask the other person where they are originally from too.

Going back to that 5 worded- question, which still needs to be answered, there have been varied responses proposed.

'I am from London'

'From my parents'

'Africa'

Or simply turn around to ask the same question too, albeit sarcastically.

I am not sure if any of these responses answer the question.

Someone suggested having a story to hand, a prepared history about who you are.

I completely agree.

I love this approach.

It is not confrontational but is highly educative, enlightening and possibly an effective solution to that age-old question.

A ready-made answer can do many things; it ensures that you are not caught off-guard, is a conversation starter and allows for intellectual discussion and education about your history.

So, for whoever is asking, here is my prepared answer.

I am Adebola Ajoke Adisa, born to Olusike and Olasupo Adekunle, from Akinmoorin, Afijio Local Government, Oyo State, South West, Yorubaland, Nigeria, West Africa, African Continent, North of the Equator, World, Planet Earth.

Selah!

Voting

If you know me, you will not think of me as a politician!

But if you truly know me you will know that I love politics!

I believe in making a positive difference in people's lives.

Politics is essential, and we cannot do without it.

The truth is that no matter how much we chat on all forms of social media or talk about it in our homes, if we do not do something, anything, no matter how small, nothing is likely to change.

I know what you are probably thinking; how has my voting made any difference in the past?

Believe me, it has.

Voting means making your choice known.

Not voting implies that you are sitting on the wall(fence if you like)

Now, who has that helped?

Humpty Dumpty too sat on the wall, and his indifference made him come tumbling down.

Seriously, people have suffered, and others have died and are dying in the process of trying to ensure that everyone gets a right to vote.

Matthew Luther King and the Suffragettes come to mind!

There may be many reasons not to vote, the elections would be rigged anyway, I am not bothered, I do not want trouble, or I do not have a valid voter's card.

They may even be valid reasons.

However, dear friends, may I encourage you to vote if you are eligible.

It is the best that you can do, and though seemingly little, it is something.

When it comes to election processes

Voting is everything that you can do.

And you should be proud of yourself.

You get to exercise your right.

And that, my friend, counts for a lot!

Resilience

Life happens!

Good and bad things happen to 'good' and 'bad' people alike.

Resilience is the ability to recover quickly from difficult situations or being able to move on from bad experiences without long-term negative consequences.

Resilient people are like rubber, and they keep 'bouncing back.'

Qualities of Resilient people

• Self-aware and honest about their strengths and weaknesses.

• They accept life for what it is!

• They are thankful for all the good that has come their way.

• Aware of and accept what they do not have control over or what they cannot change.

• They love and protect themselves from situations and people who could hurt them.

- Ready to learn, and they do not give up!
- They are ready to be firm when they need to be.
- They work in teams, share their burdens and are good team players.
- They keep their friends, mentors, supporters close to them.

How can we develop resilience?

In-born; some people are born with a lot of resilience. Childhood experiences and influences also contribute to our level of resilience.

Developed/Cultivated; our adult experiences and losses may help build our ability to be resilient if we allow them to. However, this may need to be deliberately studied and learnt.

Like rubber, we all have our elastic limits.

Developing resilience when faced with bad situations

Do not be in denial. Accept the situation for what it is.

Put things into perspective.

Do not take things too personally.

Cry if you must but avoid dwelling in a pity party.

Give yourself time to recover.

Do not give up!

Surround yourself with resilient people and learn from them, ask them what they are doing right.

Trying again

Allow yourself to fail but try again.

We can find ways of not doing things by trying.

Trying also informs us about better ways of doing things.

Looking Back

Time makes things appear clear and brighter!

The benefit of time is like the experience one has after squinting for so long, then upon wearing the perfect prescription lenses, suddenly everything becomes more focused.

So, I found myself at the same spot where I was robbed almost sixteen years ago!

Victoria Coach Station.

It was the end of my first voyage to the United Kingdom, Jand our slang for London.

It had been such a lovely trip.

My grandad(may his soul rest in peace)

Picked me up from Heathrow and drove me down to Leicester

I loved every bit of that month-long adventure.

A brief introduction to the health service of the United Kingdom, the NHS.

It paved the way for me to work in the NHS only a few years later.

I remember my friend's friendly face, only for a day

Then she had to leave too.

I also remember her warm, cosy blue and brown jumpers

I felt a bit lonely, but only for a day or two.

I enjoyed shopping in the vast mall and buzzing market

I loved sitting in the cinemas.

Watching blockbusters

It was the year of 'Love Actually.'

I loved KFC, and not McDonald's.

That love has since switched places.

Everything was so cheap.

I remember a big pack of fish and chips wrapped in white paper cost just £2.20.

No joke, it lasted several days on end

I was going home with a huge box full of new 'baffs,' new clothing.

It seemed all good until I travelled back to London on the National Express.

After a brief distraction whilst I was making a phone call, thieves made away with my black bag containing my passport.

Oh my God, I thought my world ended.

It felt like it had.

I was due back at university and did not want to be in 'trouble'.

But my grandad came to the rescue.

He took me down to the Nigerian House.

And we left with my ETC(Emergency Travel Certificate)

That temporary sadness and deep sorrow

Is almost faded from my memory

I miss my grandad

But I am also no longer feeling as sad as I was when he died,

Time heals!

Do not give up.

Feeling Stuck?

You've heard the phrase being between the devil and the deep blue sea!

Sometimes you feel stuck

You can't move forward or go backwards

Decisions may be out of your hands.

It does happen to the best of us, if not everyone.

That is the first good news

That you're not alone.

You are not a weird species.

Someone says, why can't you leave?

The truth is there are situations which you can't simply leave.

Maybe you can, but what if you really can't?

So, what do you do when you feel stuck?

• Assess the situation and know it inside out.

Then you will be better able to decide what you need to

do.

- Ask yourself if a change is an option?

  Change is often a good thing

  So why not try to do something else if possible

  It may be a new career or business plan or a new goal.

- If change is not an option, then maybe it's time to accept the situation and face your fears. I know that it's easier said than done, but we already know that running away from this isn't a listed option here

- You may need to let go of a few things for a while.

- Accept your weaknesses.

  Don't despair even if you cannot do anything about it.

  Avoid exaggerating your weaknesses and, that is not to say that you're ignoring them.

- Look inward, what have you got?

  It could be your faith, inner strength, money, friends, or family support etc.

  Consolidate your strengths.

- Whilst waiting for answers, add more value to yourself, a course, diploma, training etc.

- Keep evaluating the situation because it may have changed, and it may be time to step away or leave.

- Whatever you do, do not give up, you may not be moving just yet, but not giving up is progress.

- Time, time, time!

  We've all heard that time is a healer and, isn't it just.

  If you're still standing by then, you'll eventually find out that every situation has a time limit and therefore has an ending, no matter how long.

  I've been there, may even still be there, so I know!

Weighing Loss

The day before, I had spent the whole day preparing four
articles.
Due to a glitch on an app, a full day's worth of work was
gone.
Every single one of them!
Not only that, but all my written ideas went along too!
My goals, future write up topics, ideas for new books, and
to-do lists
Everything was gone
Poof, like smoke in the air
As soon as I realised what had happened
I wanted to cry
I very nearly did
I became irritable
I felt distraught
I spent the rest of the day trying to recover everything
So far, I have not managed to
But I am no longer sad
I have weighed the loss
And realised that it is not enough to cripple me

No, never

I could not help but compare with worse scenarios

Many have lost weightier things, money, love, relationships

and marriages, months, years of their lives, and sadly even

lives.

Sometimes through a glitch

At times though human errors

Sometimes they are never able to recover

Recently, a man was released from prison

He already spent 36 years in prison for stealing $50.

Fifty Dollars

Only fifty dollars o!

He had no lawyer to plead his case!

I cannot fathom it!

But that is life.

We do not live in a fair world

Things do not always go according to plan

There are often ups and, there are downs

Friends, you may be going through a lot

You may be ready to quit

And I am not suggesting that the loss of my notes can

compare with your loss.

No!

Still, I encourage you to pause for a moment

Stop!

Weigh that loss!

Then compare it with your gain

Compare it with the worst-case scenario

If you are reading this

You are still alive

You are here

Right here(on earth hopefully)

I have counted my losses

Life trumps my losses

I have counted my gains too

And they weigh more

Who Wants to Be a Doctor?

I enjoy my work!

I am enjoying the chance to make a difference.

I go to work praying and with a determination to give my
best

I see my profession as a privilege

One which I do not ever take for granted

I am in it to be an excellent doctor

I am in it to do my best for my patients

My parents guided me in the direction of becoming a
physician.

It is a decision that I do not regret.

People often need to make decisions about their career path
at a very young age of 16 to 18, even younger for some.

It is a very delicate age indeed, and without appropriate
guidance, this can be a very challenging step to take

One which may be prone to a lot of errors

Yet the decision often has a lasting effect on their future

The onus is on us to show clear career paths to the young
and upcoming generations
Though they still need to make their own decisions
They are better able to make them with a clear
understanding, adequate information, and mentorship

Dear young people; do come and become a doctor if

- You truly care about others.
- You dream of becoming a doctor
- You are willing to learn and happy to keep learning for
  the rest of your lives.
- You are willing to learn from your mistakes
- You are willing to work hard
- You are willing to make sacrifices of time, money,
  and emotion etc.
- You do not give up easily
- You love to serve humanity
- You want to become a leader
- You are willing to be mentored
- You are willing to work in a team and be a team player
- You are empathic or willing to learn how to be empathic
- You are not in it for the money

As a doctor, you are likely to have a stable income, but you may never become rich!

If you still wish to become a doctor, why not take the next step.

Find a reliable mentor and role model or a medical doctor near you.

Ask them if you could come along with them to work sometime, to see what they do.

If you like what you see, ask them if they are willing to mentor you.

Then go on, work hard, get into it, and do not give up.

Nothing can stop you from becoming anything you wish to become.

Remember that if you can see it, you can be it!

"I tell my students, 'When you get these jobs that you have been so brilliantly trained for, just remember that your real job is that if you are free, you need to free somebody else. If you have some power, then your job is to empower somebody else. This is not just a grab bag candy game."

-Toni Morrison

Goals

Each time you leave your house

Do you always have a destination in mind?

I am assuming that the answer is yes

I think it is the same with life goals

They could be immediate, short, or long term

They could be tiny or huge

Whatever they maybe

One of the most important principles

Is to identify each goal

Recognise it for what it is

Be aware of what it means

One other important thing

Is to write it down

It helps you to see it for what it is

It helps you to analyse it and check if it is a SMART goal

It allows you to make plans towards achieving it

It helps you to confirm when it has been achieved.

It motivates you to move on to the next goal on your list

Knowing that you are already an achiever

So, what is your goal?

What are your goals?

Are you afraid that they are too big?

Do not be discouraged

Have you been able to identify your goal?

I challenge you to write out your goals.

Once you do that, you are walking down the right path.

Celebrating Women

Do not wait for someone else to come and speak for you.
It's you who can change the world

- **Malala Yousafzai**

Can I say that women are extraordinary?
Yet, our resilience, strengths, abilities, value, versatility,
beauty, grace, skills, and achievements often go
unrecognised even by fellow women.
Women have been put down, relegated, discriminated
against, abused, injured, and even killed for being women.
Women are generally more vulnerable, are paid far less for
the same role, valued less, shamed, blamed, their skills less
appreciated, less celebrated, passed over for promotions
and so on, for being of the female gender.
But we are already aware of these
We have even experienced it.
Yet we know that what a man can do, so can a woman!
We also know that when there is gender balance, we
promote a better and more balanced world.

How then do we start putting things right?

It starts with us, for who better understands you as a woman than a fellow woman?

We must.

Stop putting ourselves down.

Find civil and legal ways to stop people who put us down.

Appreciate ourselves more.

Show others how to appreciate us.

Teach our children to appreciate women.

Teach our girls to value themselves

Resist discrimination.

Find better ways of ensuring balance.

Recognise our inner strengths and abilities.

Come together, work as teams and build strong networks.

Become more understanding, more tolerant of fellow women and stop being quick to judge them.

Celebrate the achievements of women in our world more.

Reach out to assist women around us and support them in

any way that you can, emotionally and financially

Positively influence our men to support us in this bid to balance our world.

Help men to see that this is not a contest, but a no brainer.

The balance for better starts with every one of us.

We can do more.

We can make it happen.

We all have a job to do.

Are We There Yet?

Our lives may mimic that of a road trip gone wrong
We find ourselves asking the question
Are we there yet?
Does anyone remember that movie featuring Ice cube and
Nia Long?
Ice Cube was given the responsibility of getting Nia's two
kids to a destination and he did, oh but they nearly
destroyed him!
Our life journey can get tough and seemingly impossible
Often the easiest thing to do then is to quit, to give up.
Imagine that your patience is being tested by slow-moving
traffic, unexpected roadworks, or unforeseen accidents.

What do you then do?

Do you quit and turn around to go back home or persevere
and wait in the long queue or take a detour?
If the journey is important
Most likely, you would stay put or look for a shorter route
Life goals are often the same!

#BEINSPIRED

It would seem okay to quit if it were not all that important

It is sometimes okay to sacrifice smaller goals for bigger,

more life-defining ones

But if it is an important one

We learn to persevere

We learn to wait patiently

Or find a shorter but legal route

So, friends, do not give up just yet

Take yet another step

Drive a few more yards

If you need to, stop to refuel

Then continue the journey at your pace

Navigate the crossroads

The hills and the winding turn

Do it for you

Do it for others

The Fear of F9

One thing that I feared when I was in secondary school

Was scoring an F9 in any subject.

That is like scoring a U(unclassified) in A level.

I knew that I wanted to study Medicine

So, I was prepared to work hard and make the grades.

But for some reason, may be misguided.

I chose Further Mathematics as an optional subject.

I did not like it

I feared it, but I worked hard at it

And at first, I got by

Well, that was until the end of the first term examinations

Sat in the examination room

I realised that I had gone blank

I could not remember anything

Nothing at all

I sat for a while

Still nothing

Then I got up to inform my tutor

He told me to try again

Yet nothing

#BEINSPIRED

I scored an F9 grade in that subject

My only ever F9

But I know now that I did not fail

I only found out that I did not need Further Mathematics in
my life

It was not even a prerequisite to study Medicine

The fear of F9 got to me, but that did not signify failure

I believe that you only fail when you refuse to try

You do not fail when you have tried

Meanwhile, you may learn one way of not doing things

Then you can get up and try other ways until you succeed

I know that this may seem like an overly simplified
example

It may well be

But then, life principles are simple

If we let them be

What do you fear?

What do you think you will fail at?

How about a re-evaluation

Is it a defining path in your life?

Then I encourage you to face it and see what happens

Is it an unnecessary or optional challenge?

Then I suggest that you leave it be

But do not fail to try where you should

Always ask yourself, what is the worst thing that could happen?

Because failing would not be the worst thing

It is the lack of trying at all that would be tragic!

Embracing Change

When confronted with something different to what we are familiar with

We often hesitate and at times are reluctant to engage with it.

Change, as we all know, is inevitable.

For instance, the ageing process is a type of change.

The other week on BBC Radio 4

Some teenagers were interviewed about Artificial Intelligence(AI)

One of them said something that made me think.

"AI is coming for sure, indeed is here to stay

He said that there was no point in complaining or wishing that it would not come.

And as such, would it not be better if we kept looking for ways of channelling the use of it for our good. For example, in the treatment of diseases.

Change can mean different things, progress, demotion, loss, gain, a move, addition, or a reversal.

It is likely to mean that things would not stay the same.

When change comes, we sometimes passively allow it to run its course, actively engage with it or occasionally resist it.

I am not sure that there is a right or wrong way to handle change, but I think that resisting change may defeat the essence or purpose for which it came!

So over to you, what do you usually do when change happens?

Trying on Other People's Shoes

Growing up, I loved putting on my mother's size seven high heeled shoes, just for fun.

Later I wore them for real, out to events and parties, but they were always uncomfortable.

You see, I wear size eight shoes.

I have in the past also tried my sister's size nine shoes, some fit okay, but most times they slip off and can feel inconvenient.

It is often challenging to find size nine shoes at the shop And I cannot fully appreciate my sister's struggles to find her shoes.

Onikaluku lomo ibiti bata tinta lese, is a Yoruba saying which means that everyone knows where their shoes hurt.

How apt is that?

You cannot simply wave off someone else's pain and insist that their shoes do not hurt when they say that it does.

How could you when you are not the person wearing them?

I think that the saying, walking in someone else's shoes has several facets to it.

1. For instance, if you walked in someone else's shoes, a smaller size, it is likely to be very uncomfortable indeed.

2. If you walked in someone else's stilettos(shoes with very high thin heels], even if they were an exact fit, but you are usually more comfortable wearing casual loafers or trainers, then it would be a difficult, if not an impossible task.

3. If you walked along someone else's usual path in their shoes, even if they were your exact size, you might still struggle with the unfamiliarity of their journey.

In case you wondered, yes, my writing is about empathy.
To become better people, we must be empathic.
We must see and fit ourselves into other peoples' shoes,
feel their pain and struggles as if they are ours.
We may be unable to show that we care if we stand as far away as possible.

The keyword here is to try, we could at least try, but not just try a bit, we could try harder.

I know that I better understand and empathise more with patients who are going through severe vomiting in pregnancy because I went through the same.

However, we may not always go through what people may be going through, yet to support them sincerely, we need to assume their roles, life journeys, experiences, shame, pain, and loss.

At first, it may be difficult to sincerely empathise with other people, especially if they are not our family members or friends, yet we need to make deliberate attempts to do so.

After a while, it is likely to become easier, and we become better, more tolerant people as a result.

Ameyo Adadevoh

How could I ever forget the deep fear which engulfed me,
indeed, all of us when we found out that there were Ebola
cases in Nigeria.

I feared, and I was scared.

All I remembered about Ebola was what we learned at
Medical School.

How contagious and deadly it was.

But for this brave woman and her co-heroes.

It would have led to an Epidemic if not a Pandemic
outcome.

A Patriot and Professional.

Honest and Selfless.

Great-granddaughter of Herbert Macaulay.

Of the lineage of the legendary Bishop Samuel Ajayi
Crowther.

She was swift to recognise the disease and stopped patient
zero from leaving the country.

It was one of the best decisions ever made.

She and her formidable team heroically saved Nigeria and
indeed the world.

For we all know how 'Ajala travel all over the world' we are.

Ajala travel is a well-known Nigerian saying to depict someone who likes to travel, a globetrotter.

Sadly, she and others laid down their lives.

Now we can smile and even laugh in retrospect at those who spread the rumour that mere talcum powder could prevent the spread of Ebola.

She and the others gave up all for our country.

What will you give up for your country?

May the labour of our heroes past.

Never be in vain.

Rest in peace, dear esteemed senior colleague!

Rest in peace, dear heroes of Nigeria!!

Rest in Peace!!!

Book Crush

I love books, me!

My love love relationship with books began early on, but my earliest memories of this special bond were in secondary school.

It became stronger during the long break between junior and senior secondary school, just after our JSCE examinations.

When everyone else went to school or work, I was left at home, home alone.

I was bored and ended up reading everything that I could lay my hands on, novels, autobiographies, newspapers, church bulletins, even Encyclopedias.

Everything except textbooks.

I loved James Hadley Chase and Pacesetters.

I did not fancy Mills and Boon, but if stuck somewhere with no choice, they made do!

When I returned to school, my thirst for books became unquenchable.

During lessons, I remember sneaking in Pacesetter, Sweet Valley High and Danielle Steel novels in

between my Biology textbook, Modern Biology or
Goh Cheng Leong, my favourite Geography
textbook.

I would read novels whilst in class, lucky I was
never caught.

I am sure that I am not alone, who else did this?
It is confession time!

I also remember borrowing books on fixed deadlines,
for instance, I would promise to complete a book,
and return it in 2 hours just so that I could skip
the long, never-ending queue of equally desperate
fellow readers.

And I always delivered.

I think that is how I developed quick reading skills.

The last time I travelled to Nigeria, I filled one
entire suitcase with my old books, about 22kg
worth.

My luggage allowance put a restriction on how
much I could carry, and I was sad to leave some of my
books behind.

I love bookshops, that lovely, raw smell of fresh
new books!

I might not enjoy shopping for clothes, shoes, and

bags, but books, oh yes, please!

Now we have easier access to books, libraries,

bookshops, e-books, book fairs, book clubs.

Reading books opens the world and brings it closer

to you.

So, when last did you read a book?

What is your favourite genre?

Do you like thrillers, science, romance, crime,

history, or autobiographies?

Do you prefer paperbacks, e-books, or audiobooks?

Do not give any more excuses.

Find out more about the world around you.

Discover something new.

Read a book today.

Mentors

One of the things that I have come to realise is that we
need mentors.
We should not have to go through life without
checks, and balances guiding what we do and how
we do it.
A mentor is an adviser, a teacher.
Having mentors can mean different things at
different milestones in our lives.
For instance, our parents and or guardians mentor
us early in life.
At school, university, or vocational training,
a mentor can mean our trainer, supervisor, or teacher.
Mentors are people who have gained the experience
that we need, through time, tests, and practice.
In a trainee-trainer relationship, you could save a lot
of time and heartache because your trainer can
teach you the ropes, how to arrive at short cuts and
how to avoid making the same mistakes that they or
others have made.

Even when we become qualified or become bosses, we still need mentors.

No matter how successful we become, there would always be someone more experienced, and even more successful and I am not speaking mainly about financial success here.

There is always someone that we can learn from.

A good mentor-mentee relationship is a mutually beneficial one.

Key attributes to look out for in mentors

• Patient
• Respectful
• Trustworthy
• Willing to teach you
• Not jealous of you
• Disciplined(may be very strict, but is kind-hearted)
• Believes in you
• Supports you

- Committed to you
- Respects confidentiality
- Professional

Attributes of a good mentee.

- Humble
- Willing to learn
- Determined
- Disciplined
- Time conscious
- Motivated
- Honest
- Respectful
- Committed
- Pro-active
- Goal focused
- Will follow your advice

Remember that these are not exhaustive lists.

Do you have a mentor, or are you a mentor?

If you ever find a great mentor, never let go of them!

Keep Going, Don't Stop!

Yesterday, it felt like almost all the traffic lights
along my way home turned red!
Even the one that I cannot recall ever stopping me in
my last two years of driving along that road.
It felt like all the possible obstacles got thrown in as
bonuses, including slow-moving cars and drivers
who did not seem to be in a hurry to get to their
destinations.
It felt like forever!
But guess what?
I made it and got home in time.
I know how I love to simplify things, but yes,
life's journey can feel like that too.
It can feel like all the odds are stacked up, against
you.
Every obstacle lined up along your path, threatening
to prevent you from reaching your goal.
And the only reasonable thing to do is to quit!
Though it seems like the logical thing to do.
Friends let's not quit!

Bypass, U-turn, slow down, divert, temporarily
stop, even reverse, if need be, do everything else, but
do not quit.
Instead, focus on that goal.
No one said that life was easy.
Or that reaching our goals would be a smooth sail.
Remember that failure is not always the lack of
success.
But often a result of not trying at all.
If we keep trying hard and for long enough.
Something usually gives.
So, do not quit
Keep going!

#BEINSPIRED

Part 3; Poetry and Quotes

Here we have some selected poems and quotes.

#BEINSPIRED

Life's Good!

Life's good

Live it to the fullest

Perceive it

It gives so much hope

Love each day

Touch it

Enjoy every moment

Own it

Help someone to live it

Never limit it

Don't restrict it

Life is a gift

Cherish it

Live it to the fullest

Remember you don't own it

You can't create it

Protect it

You got it free

Breathe it

Recharge it

#BEINSPIRED

Walk it with someone

That special someone

Teach them to love it

Don't snuff it out

Stop!

Don't pollute it

Value it

Live it to the fullest

Train in it

Bless each day you see it

Feel it

Do not abandon it

Experience it

Be it

Birth it

Never kill it

Grow it

Nurture it

Feed it till it blossoms

Clothe it

It's yours to adore

Be thankful for it

Shelter it

Life is everyone you meet

Celebrate it

Life is good

Live it to the fullest!

This Class of 400

Everyone complains

Very few have any hope

Scarce kind words

About this class

This class of 400

This Hall is too stuffy

You're unlikely to make it

Who admitted you all?

How do we cope with you?

It's all too chaotic

This class of 400

Like a multitude

Of thunderous noise

Diverse in her ways

Shapes forms and sizes

Therein lies her beauty

This class of 400

Determined to make it

United we stand

Not to be outdone

Nor stepped upon

This class of 400

We shall survive

Come what may

We will make it

Against all the odds

This class of 400

We are special

Together we strive

Onwards to the mark

And towards the goal

This class of 400

Doubts may arise

We are undeterred

We soon spread our wings

Liberated

Ready to soar

This class of 400

Shinning bright

Against a dark sky

As stars that we are!

Dedicated to my medical school class, the UCH 2000 set.

(University College Hospital Ibadan, Oyo State, Nigeria).

Be Forgetful

You hear people say to forgive and forget

You say I'll forgive

I will never forget

Be forgetful

Oh, to be childlike

Haven't you seen them?

Pure and content

How easily they forget

How freely they love and give their all

Be forgetful

Be forgetful of the hurtful past

The hurtful present and future

Be forgetful

Be forgetful of the unkind actions of many

Their haughty looks and deeds

Be forgetful

Be forgetful of the wrongs done to you

From near or from far

Be forgetful of the misdeeds of friends

Of acquaintances

Self-declared enemies

Be forgetful

Be forgetful of past failures

Near misses and miscarriage of justice

Be forgetful

Be forgetful of the waiting periods

Unanswered prayers and petitions

Be forgetful

Be forgetful because it doesn't cost a thing

No that is not true at all

Is it?

I won't lie

It will cost you to forgive and to forget

But it'll cost you more if you don't

Be forgetful

Being forgetful is a deliberate act

You must remember to forget

In forgetting is forgiveness

In forgetting you truly forgive

Be forgetful

Forgive completely

Wipe the slate clean

Forget totally

#BEINSPIRED

Start over

Be forgetful

In forgetting, you are loving yourself

Therein also lies healing

In forgetting you are declaring yourself free

Free from the bondage of unforgiveness

Be forgetful

Don't be a hoarder of misdeeds

Don't store up your hurts

Let them go

They ain't worth the hassle

Be forgetful

Clear up your hearts

Clean up your soul

Embrace your sanity

Be forgetful

For how can one truly forgive?

Without forgetting

Be forgetful

Ise Ni Ogun Ise

On work ethics!

One of the earliest poems I learned was in Yoruba.

Ise Ni Ogun Ise (Work is the solution to poverty)

by J.F. Odunjo

I still know it by heart

I have taken the liberty of translating it, so any

errors in the English translation will be you know

whose!

Happy reading

'Ise l'ogun ise

(Work is the solution to poverty)

Mura s'ise ore mi

(My friend, do work hard)

Ise la fi n'deni giga

(Work gives us the chance to attain great heights)

Bi a ko ba reni feyin ti

(If we do not have anyone to rely on)

Bi ole l'ari

(We appear to be lazy)

Bi a ko ba reni gbekele

(If we do not have any support)

A tera mo'se eni

(We may need to strive harder)

Iya re le lowo lowo

(Your mother might be wealthy)

Baba re le lesin lekan

(Your father may have massive properties)

Bi o ba gbo'ju l'ewon

(If you depend only on them)

O te tan ni mo so fun o

(Trouble awaits you)

Ohun ti a ko ba ji'ya fun,

(Whatever we obtain without hardwork)

Se ki ipe lowo;

(It does not often last)

Ohun ti a ba fara sise fun,

(Whatever you obtain through hardwork)

Nii pe lowo eni.

(We usually own for life)

Apa lara

(Your arms are all you have)

Igunpa niyekan

(You can rely on your elbows)

B'aye ba n'fe o loni

(Everyone may love you now)

Bi o ba lowo lowo

(If you remain wealthy)

Aye a ma fe o lola

(They will keep loving you)

Tabi ki o wa ni'po atata

(Or if you are a celebrity)

Aye a ye o si terin-terin

(The world will celebrate you)

Je k'o de'ni tin rago

(Wait till you become poor)

Aye a ma yinmu si o

(Then the world will mock you)

Eko si'nso ni d'oga

(Being educated gives you a chance to soar)

Mura ki o ko dara dara

(Ensure that you obtain the best out of formal

learning)

Bi o si r'opo eniyan

(And if you see the crowd)

Ti won f'eko s'erin rinrin

(Making a mockery of education)

Dakun ma f'ara we won

(Please do not join them)

Iya n'bo fun'omo ti ko gbon

(Suffering is the reward to the foolhardy)

Ekun n'be fun'omo to nsa kiri

(Sorrow soon catches up with the wayward)

Ma f'owuro sere ore mi

(Do not waste your productive years)

Mura si'se ojo'nlo

(Work hard now because time waits for no man)'

So, this was true in the past, my question is, is it

still true?

Is this still the reality today?

Is it likely to be true for the coming generation?

What do you think?

PS

A version of the English translation has been

making rounds on social media.

Kudos to the original translator.

A Run in The Park

A flight of birds perfecting their flying skills

Conducting rhythmic mix of tweets

The willow tree sitting on its throne by the river

The cool still lake almost at freezing point.

Paddling ducks rippling the water

The talking parrot, saying 'morning'.

Squirrels playing like kids in a playground

The dog loyal to its owner striding along

The smoky mist giving off a picturesque view

The cool air of nature caressing my face

The sun high up in all its glory.

And my friend and I

Blessed to savour it all.

Savour the Moment

It's been a glorious summer

One could decide to enjoy every bit of it.

Bask in the heat and shine of the sun

Or one could worry about how cold the coming

winter would likely be

Or how chilly the snow and minus temperature

would bite

Either way, what's coming is coming.

Nothing you do, say or feel would change that.

Summer and Winter

Springtime and Harvest

They are sure to have their own time.

It is what it is

It is what we have

We can choose to enjoy it all.

It's a choice

It really is!

I will enjoy it

Will you do too?

Will you choose to?

What do You See When You See Me?

I cannot see myself even if I wanted to

And if I try hard

I can just about see the edge of my nose

I may be able to see my reflection in the clear water

But you see me better than any mirror could ever do

And what you see is what you get

What do you see when you see me?

Do you see my beautiful smile?

Or my kind heart

Do you see a hardworking woman?

A good friend or colleague

Or do you just see the colour of my skin?

Or how my accent is different?

What do you see when you see me?

Do you see that I am human just like you?

Who should not be denied privileges?

Or an immigrant who should return to Africa

Do you see the descendants of slaves?

Or someone who does not deserve a seat at the table

What do you see when you see me?

Do you allow the colour of my skin?

Create a divide

Life versus death

Wealth versus poverty

Employed versus jobless

Educated versus school dropout

Entrepreneur versus crushed dreams

Politician versus the downtrodden masses

Isn't it interesting that none of us has a say?

About what the colour of skin we are born in is

We were not there

Well, for one, I was not present.

When mum and dad decided to get together,

and make me

I bet you were not there either!

Even if it crossed my mind to

I cannot even change that I'm black.

So why am I being judged on a characteristic?

That I cannot change

In the wake of the killing of George Floyd

In a video which was all levels of evil

I keep saying that I wish I'd never seen it

Then it is apparent that we all need to

Never to unsee it

Lest we forget

It has become more important

That we evaluate ourselves

Each one of us

Black and white

Next time you look at me

Please see that I am human

That I have equal rights as you

Deserve the same opportunities

That I have a lot to offer

Just as you do too

May this death not be in vain

Trying

"Trying is not failure. However, the lack of trying may well be!"

- Adebola Adisa

Life is a Kaleidoscope

"Life itself is a Kaleidoscope."

-Adebola Adisa

Everyone has a Book in Them!

"Everyone has a book in them. You have a book in you. Write it."

-Adebola Adisa

Life's Struggles

"I can guarantee that whatever it is that you are facing is not new.

I can also guarantee that it is possible to survive whatever you're facing.

I know this because whilst there might be millions of problems in the world, they are only a fraction of the billions of people who have passed through, are in this world, and survived whatever they faced."

-Adebola Adisa

Legacy

"In striving for excellence, ensure that you make a positive impact so that you can be a person of lasting value."

-Adebola Adisa

Time

"Time makes things clearer and brighter!
The benefit of time is like the experience one has after squinting for so long, then upon wearing the perfect prescription lenses, suddenly everything comes into focus."

-Adebola Adisa

Goals

"If we set our own goals and standards, it means that we can always unset, and reset them."

-Adebola Adisa

#BEINSPIRED

Conclusion

I sincerely hope that you have found my book #Beinspired, inspiring.

If so, kindly write your review on amazon.

Also, tell others about it so that they too can be inspired.

Don't forget to read my other books 'The Magic of Destiny,' 'Kaleidoscopes,' 'How to Write your book 101,' 'Dr Fact's Continents of the World,' and 'Dr Fact's Planets of the Solar System'.

I thank you !

#BEINSPIRED

About the Author

Dr Adebola Adisa is a wife, mum, GP, inspirational speaker and author of six books.

Adebola promotes healthy living through articles, health topics, poetry, and other inspirational writing on her social media pages and is the face of the NHS England #helpustohelpyou campaign.

She is the founder of Brave Hearts North East CIC, a group in the North East of England. The group support their community by fundraising for book and food donations, promoting holistic health through sports, health talks and participation in the yearly Race for life organised by Cancer Research UK (CRUK). They have recently launched a mentorship program for secondary school pupils in Darlington.

She is a STEM Ambassador, school Governor, and a Black Women in Health (BWIH) executive. BWIH actively supports black women in medicine and healthcare.

Adebola stays active by gardening and enjoys spending time with her family, cooking and exploring new dishes.

Adebola believes that everyone has a book in them and is passionate about assisting them on their journey to writing it!

Her life motto is #beinspired.